Sharks

by Helen Orme

Ransom

D1144307

Trailblazers

Sharks
by Helen Orme
Educational consultant: Helen Bird

Illustrated by Mik Brown

Published by Ransom Publishing Ltd.
51 Southgate Street, Winchester, Hants. SO23 9EH
www.ransom.co.uk

ISBN   978 1841167 797 2
First published in 2009

Illustrations copyright © 2009 Mik Brown
'Get the Facts' section - images copyright: Bull Sharks - Ian Scott, Andy Murch; Great White Sharks - Terry Goss, Bart Coenders, Mila Zinkova; Tiger Shark, Great White Shark, Caribbean Reef Shark - Chris Dascher; racehorse - David Maczkowiack; bathing in River Ganges - Ilya Mauter; Shark's Fin soup - Chee Hong; shark fins - U.S. National Oceanic and Atmospheric Administration; oil platform - Mayumi Terao; cows - Peter Clark; hippo - Peter Malsbury; shark silhouette - Jan Dabrowski; fish eating fish - Miroslaw Pieprzyk; USSR stamp - A. Sdobnikov; Whale Shark - Zak Wolf; blood - Eduard Härkönen.

Sharks

Contents

Sharks

Get
the
facts

Danger – sharks!

First, find the shark!

Great White Sharks have a white belly and a grey back. This makes it hard for the shark's **prey** to see it.

Great Whites are found in the sea where the water temperature is between 12 and 30 degrees centigrade.

One of the **best places** to find Great Whites is around **Dyer Island, South Africa**.

A **Great White** tagged in 2005 and named 'Nicole' **swam** from **South Africa** to **Australia**, and back.

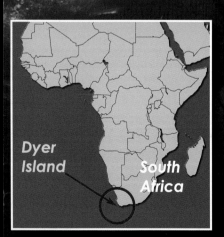

Dyer Island

South Africa

The round trip was about **22,000 km.**

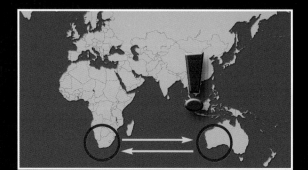

The **Basking Shark** is the second biggest fish in the shark family.

Bull Sharks swim in fresh water and can be found a long way up rivers.

The **Spiny Dogfish** is the longest-living type of shark. It can live for up to **100 years**.

What's on *your* stamps?

The **Whale Shark** is the largest fish in the world. It can grow to over **16 metres** long.

Killer sharks

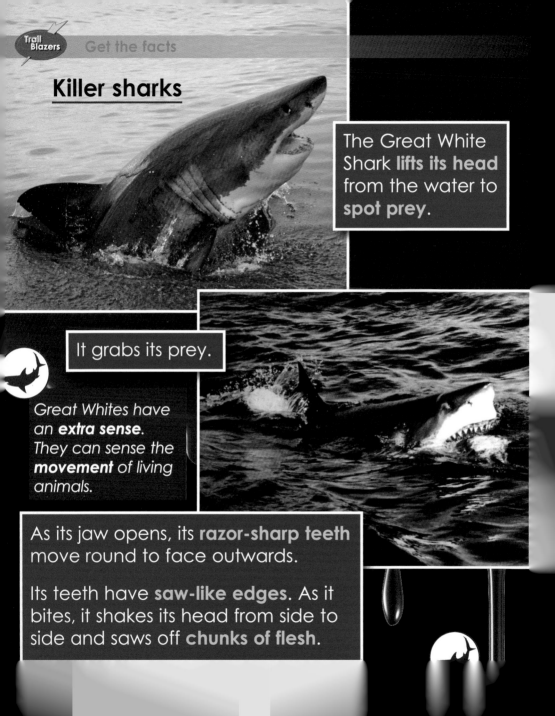

The Great White Shark **lifts its head** from the water to **spot prey.**

It grabs its prey.

*Great Whites have an **extra sense.** They can sense the **movement** of living animals.*

As its jaw opens, its **razor-sharp teeth** move round to face outwards.

Its teeth have **saw-like edges.** As it bites, it shakes its head from side to side and saws off **chunks of flesh.**

The shark will take **one bite**, then back off.

It **waits** for the prey **to die**.

Great Whites often **hunt** close to **sunrise** as they are **hard to see** at this time.

This is **safer** for the shark. It doesn't need to get into a **fight** with an animal which might fight back.

This is a good time for a **swimmer** to **escape** – if he has friends to help.

One man **fought off** a 10 ft Great White by **poking** the shark's **eye** with his **fingers**.

Be very afraid!

It's not *always* me!

This might be the **real killer:**

A Bull Shark!

Male Bull Sharks are **very fierce.** They don't always behave in ways that people expect.

They **hunt alone**, often in shallow waters. They are probably responsible for **more attacks** on people than **Great White Sharks.**

They like to eat fish, other sharks, rays, dolphins and even land animals (when they can catch them!).

One swam up the **Brisbane River** in **Queensland,** Australia, and attacked a **racehorse.**

Faster!!

Others have swum up the **River Ganges**, in **India**, where they have attacked bathers.

Did you know?

 There have been **sharks** on Earth for **over 400 million years**. There were sharks even **before the dinosaurs**.

 A giant prehistoric shark, the **Megalodon**, lived between **16** and **1.6 million years ago**.

It was probably the **largest meat-eating fish** ever.

We know about it from **fossil teeth**. They are like the teeth of the Great White Shark, but much bigger (up to 17cm long!).

The fossilised jaw of a Megalodon.

 Great White Sharks are known to eat objects that they can't digest, such as **large planks of wood**.

Sharks' skeletons are **cartilage**, not bone.
(Cartilage is the stuff your nose is made of.)

This **rots away** when a shark dies, so
the **main shark fossils** are **teeth**.

Sharks **never stop growing**.

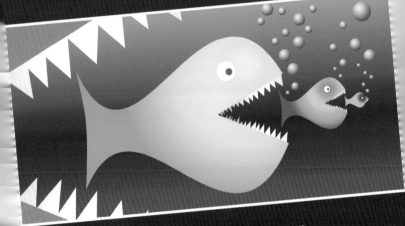

Great White Sharks can
detect one drop of **blood** in
gallons of **water**.

There are over 350 known **species** of shark.

Some sharks **must swim** all the time,
or their bodies would **sink**.

What is the most dangerous?

All sharks can be **dangerous** if you annoy them; but some sharks are more likely to attack people than others.

The most dangerous sharks are the **Bull Shark**, the **Great White Shark** and the **Tiger Shark**.

Sharks aren't as dangerous as some other animals:

DON'T PANIC!

In 2008 there were 59 reported shark attacks, but only 4 people died.

One of the most dangerous animals is the **hippopotamus**. In **Africa** there are up to 1,000 hippo attacks in a year, with as many as 150 people killed.

Worldwide, **cows** kill over 100 people a year.

In **Australia** car drivers have to watch out for **kangaroos**, which cause up to 500 car accidents with over 25 deaths in a year.

So what is the most dangerous creature of all?

The **mosquito**, which kills over a million people every year.

15

Be kind to sharks

Sharks are in danger.

Sharks have only a few **young** and those **mature slowly**.

Parent sharks don't look after their babies and so the babies might be eaten by a bigger shark.

Shark's fin soup is popular in some countries. The fishermen don't bother to keep the whole shark. They **cut** the **fins** off the **live sharks** and then throw the animals back into the sea.

Shark fins.

People

The biggest threat to sharks is from people.

Millions of sharks are caught accidentally by people fishing for tuna.

Pollution

Pollution affects all marine life, including sharks.

Protection

In 1991 **South Africa** became the first country in the world to protect the **Great White Shark** by law. Several other countries have done the same.

In the U.K. **Basking Sharks** are protected.

17

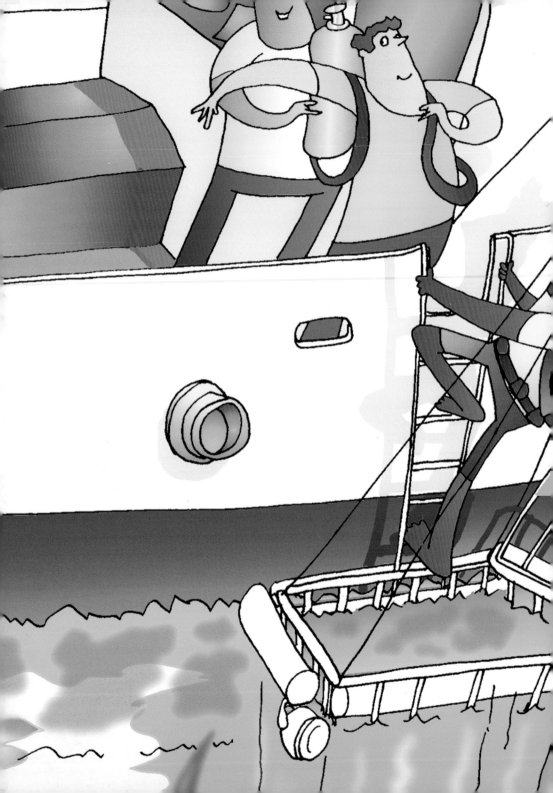

Swimming
with
Sharks

Chapter 1:
A great birthday present

It was my birthday present. I'd always loved sharks. I went to the local Sea World every birthday when I was younger. My friends got fed up with it, but not me.

Never.

But this was special. Mum and dad paid for me and my mate Danny to go swimming with sharks – in South Africa!

Well, it *was* my eighteenth.

And it wasn't just *any* old sharks. It was the best of the lot – Great Whites!

We had a few days before the shark day. We had to do some training. They checked that we knew how to dive.

Then they told us about the sharks. Dyer Island is the best place in the world to see Great Whites.

They showed us the cage. The guy said it would be safe even if the shark decided to bite it! I asked how many sharks had tried, but he just laughed.

'Don't worry – I'm still here!'

Chapter 2:
The cage

The cage floats under the boat. It doesn't go deep because the sharks feed near the surface.

They take a seal out for bait – just to get the sharks interested.

We climbed down. Then they lowered the cage. It was amazing – really clear.

They threw the seal into the water and we waited.

But not for long!

At first it was just one. We were close enough to the surface for the light to make patterns on the skin of the shark.

We watched the first one carefully. It swam by. Close by.

Then it saw the seal. It moved so fast. It snapped up the seal and blood gushed out into the sea.

Almost straight away two more sharks appeared. They came up right under the cage.

Then one of them came up close. We could feel the cage rock as it swam past.

Chapter 3:
Blood

Danny put his arm out. They told us not to put any part of our body outside the cage but I think he just couldn't help himself.

He put his hand on the side of the shark. He moved his arm one way, then back again. And that's where it all started.

One way the shark's skin feels smooth. But the other way – well, it's like brushing your fingers over broken glass.

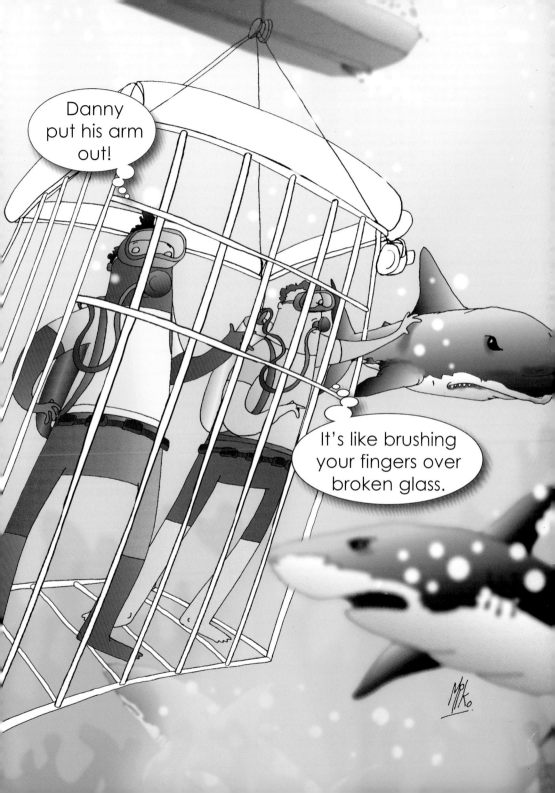

Danny pulled his arm back. He held up his hand and showed me.

Blood!

Not a lot, but any blood is a disaster if you are close to sharks. Once they get the scent of blood in the water – well, they go mad. They won't give up until they find out where it's coming from.

The shark had turned. It was heading back towards the cage.

It was a big one. And it wasn't alone.

Chapter 4:
Holding on

I looked up. It wasn't far to the surface and I knew they were watching.

The cage was moving. Had they seen? Were they bringing us up?

No! It was the sharks.

They were swimming round and round. The way they moved was different. Not slow and lazy like before but faster, more frantic, jerky.

The cage rocked. A head was trying to get through. I could see teeth. Rows and rows of teeth. Razor sharp.

More blood. It had got Danny!

The cage was moving again. Upwards now. But the shark was holding on.

I punched it. As hard as I could. Right in the eye. I punched again.

It let go! Danny's arm was a mess.

We were still moving up. The sharks were moving too. Away from us. Towards the seal bodies falling through the water.

We were out of the water. Out of the cage, being pulled onto the deck.

Safe, at last ...

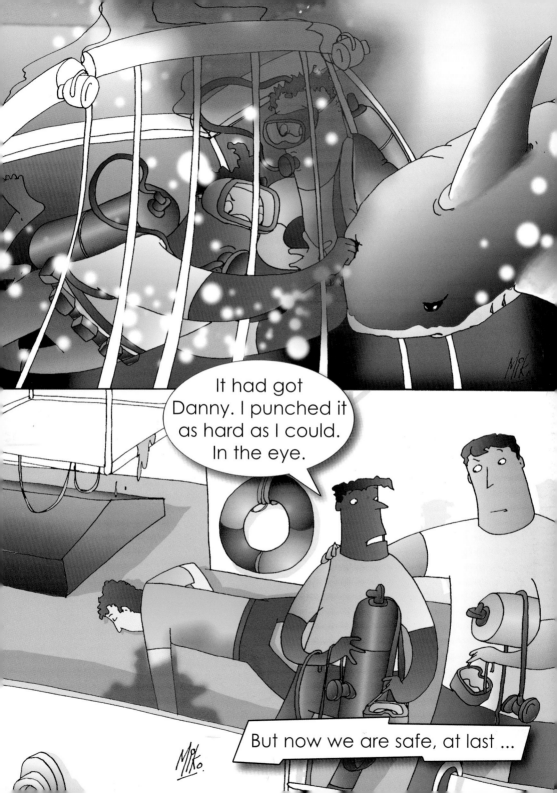

Sharks word check

Basking Shark	pollution
Bull Shark	prehistoric
cartilage	prey
fossil	species
Great White Shark	Spiny Dogfish
marine biologist	temperature
Megalodon	Whale Shark
outline	